THE START AND END OF THE KOREAN WAR

HISTORY BOOK OF FACTS
CHILDREN'S HISTORY

BABY PROFESSOR
EDUCATION KIDS

The Korean War occurred from June 25, 1950 to July 27, 1953 between communist North Korea and South Korea. This war was the first conflict resulting from the Cold War since the Soviet Union was in support of North Korea and the United States was in support of South Korea. The war came to an end without much resolution. The countries remain divided today and North Korea continues to be under rule of a communist regime. In this book, we will be learning more about this war.

LEADERS

Kim Il-sung was the leader as well as the Prime Minister of North Korea. Choi Yong-kun was the chief commander of North Korea.

KIM IL-SUNG

Syngman Rhee was South Korea's President and their army was led by Chung Il-kwon. General Douglas MacArthur led the United States Army and the United Nations' forces.

Harry Truman was the US President when the war started and Dwight D. Eisenhower was President as the war came to an end.

COUNTRIES INVOLVED IN THE WAR

Supporters of North Korea included the People's Republic of China as well as the Soviet Union. Great Britain, the United States, as well as the United Nations supported South Korea.

SOUTH KOREA AND NORTH KOREA BORDER

PRIOR TO THE KOREAN WAR

The Korean Peninsula was a part of Japan before World War II. After WWII, it had to be split up. The Northern half of this peninsula went under control of the Soviet Union and the United States took control of the Southern half of the peninsula. The 38th parallel was the dividing point between the Northern half and the Southern half.

Two separate states eventually would form -- North Korea under a communist government with Kim Il-sung as its leader; South Korea under a capitalist government under Syngman Rhee's rule.

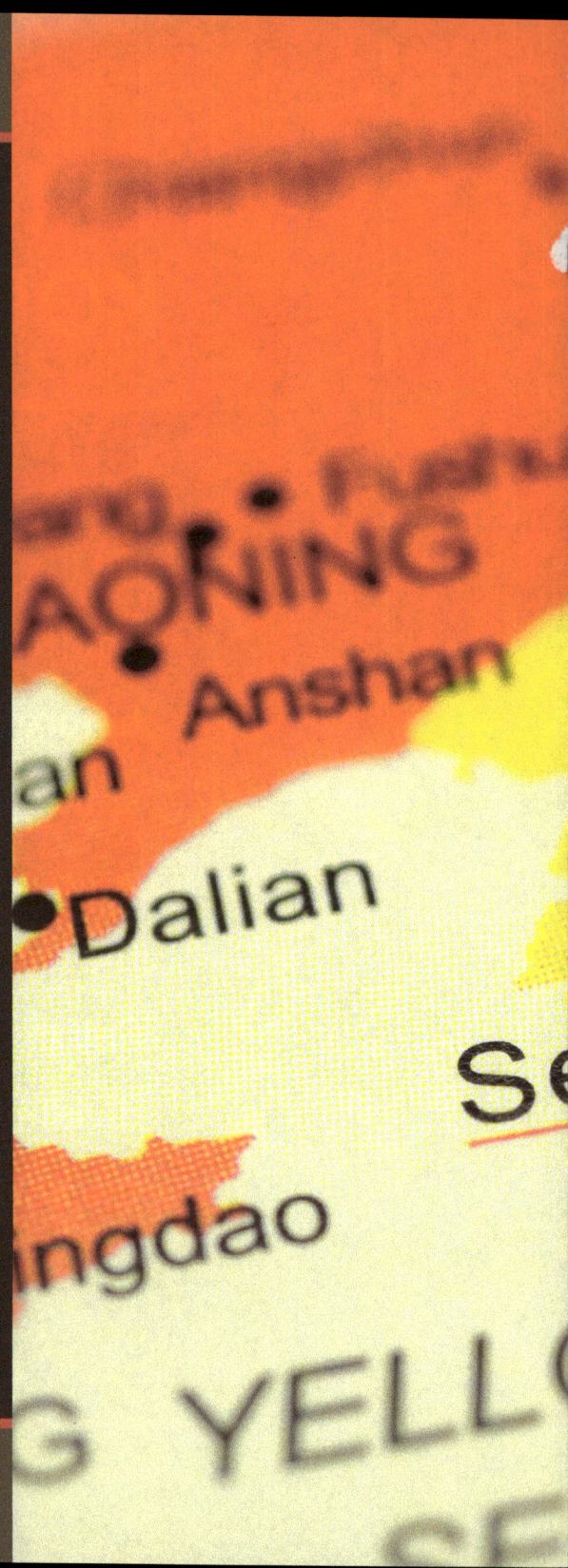

NORTH
KOREA
○ Pyongyang

oul ○ SOUTH
KOREA

Taegu
Pusan

Kita Kyushu

O

SEA

Kobe

Hiroshi

K

KOREAN DEMILITARIZED ZONE

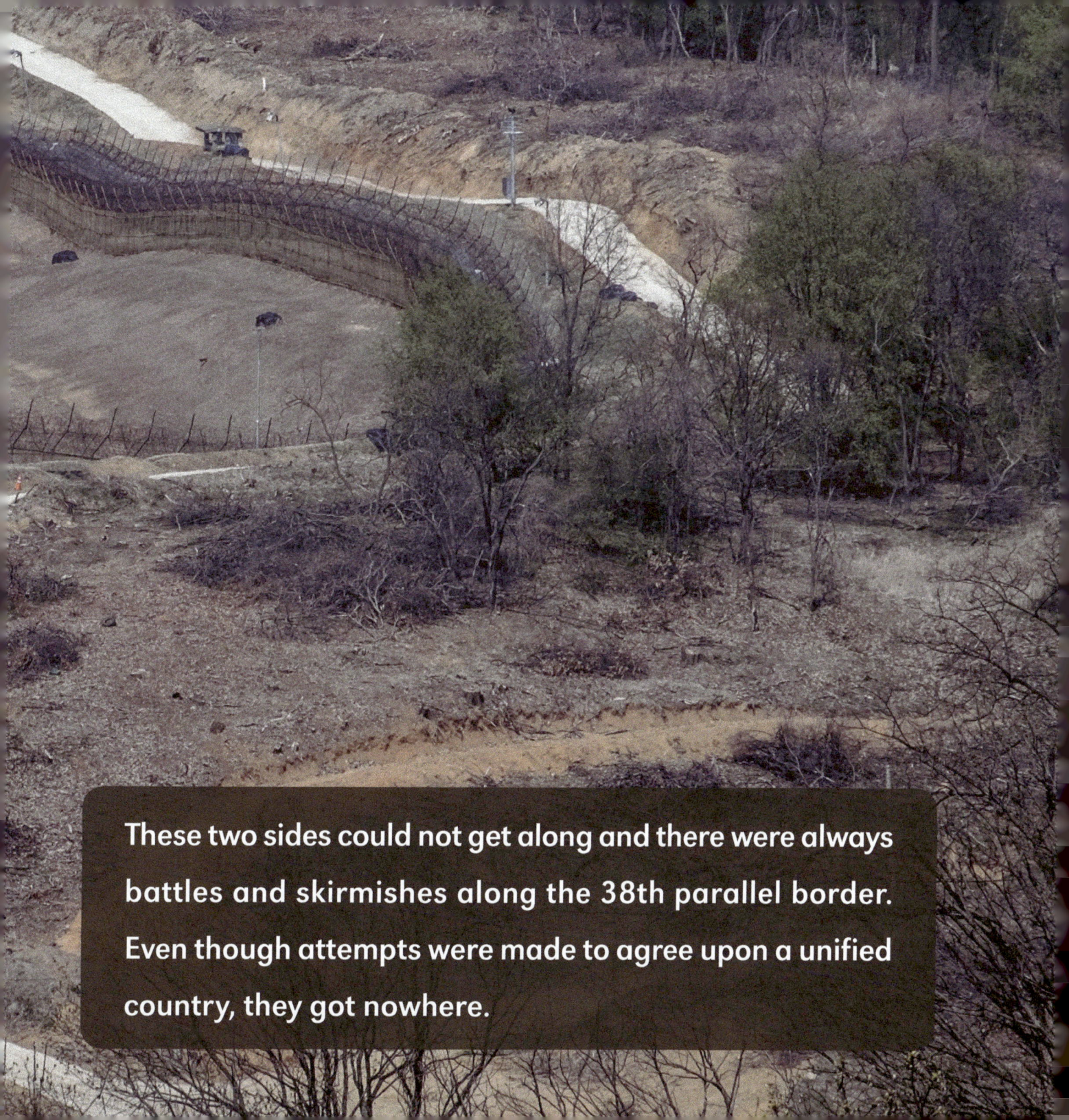

These two sides could not get along and there were always battles and skirmishes along the 38th parallel border. Even though attempts were made to agree upon a unified country, they got nowhere.

NORTH KOREA ATTACKS SOUTH KOREA

North Korea decided to invade South Korea on June 25, 1950. Once the Army of South Korea fled, the United Nations' forces came to assist. Most of the forces of the United Nations were provided by the United States. The government of South Korea soon occupied only a small part of the southern tip of Korea.

AERIAL BOMBING ON NORTH KOREA

The United Nations was simply attempting to defend South Korea at first, however, President Truman chose to go on the offensive after the first summer of battle. President Truman advised the war now was to liberate North Korea from communistic rule.

BATTLE OF INCHON

During the Battle of Inchon, General MacArthur led the forces of the United Nations on attack. This battle was successful and he was now able to move in and push back most of North Korea's army. Before long, he took control over the city of Seoul and South Korea back up towards the 38th parallel.

GENERAL MATTHEW RIDGWAY

CHINA

General MacArthur, continuing to be aggressive, pushed the North Koreans towards the northern border, all the way. The Chinese, however, were not happy about this and proceeded to send their army and enter the war. President Truman then replaced General MacArthur with General Matthew Ridgway.

BACK TO THE 38TH PARALLEL

Slightly north of the 38th parallel, Ridgway strengthened the border. These two sides battled here during the rest of the war.

North Korea attacked the south at varying points and the United Nations army retaliated in trying to stop more attacks.

DWIGHT EISENHOWER

END OF THE WAR

As negotiations would continue during most of the war, President Truman didn't want to seem weak. Once Eisenhower was instated as president, he was more agreeable to bargain to end this war.

A treaty was signed on July 17, 1953, that would bring an end to the war. Most things remained the same. Both countries would continue to be independent and the 38th parallel continued as the border.

However, they placed a 2-mile demilitarized zone which acted as a buffer with hopes of preventing wars in the future.

KOREAN DEMILITARIZED ZONE

THE COLD WAR

An extended time of tension between the Eastern Europe communist countries and the Western World democracies was known as the Cold War. The Soviet Union commanded Eastern Europe and the United States commanded the west. The two countries were known as superpowers. While these two superpowers never declared war on one another officially, they would indirectly fight in proxy wars, the arms race, as well as the space race.

The beginning of the Cold War was in 1945, soon after World War II came to an end. While the Soviet Union was known to be an important part of the Allied Powers, there was much mistrust between the Soviet Union and the remaining allies. The Allies became concerned with Joseph Stalin's brutal leadership as well as the movement of communism.

VIGILANCE
STATE

COLD WAR BUNKER

In 1991, the Cold War ended with the Soviet Union collapse.

PROXY WARS

Often being fought among the Soviet Union and the superpowers of the United States, were proxy wars, which were wars that were fought among other countries, however, each side would get the support of a different superpower.

VIETNAM WAR

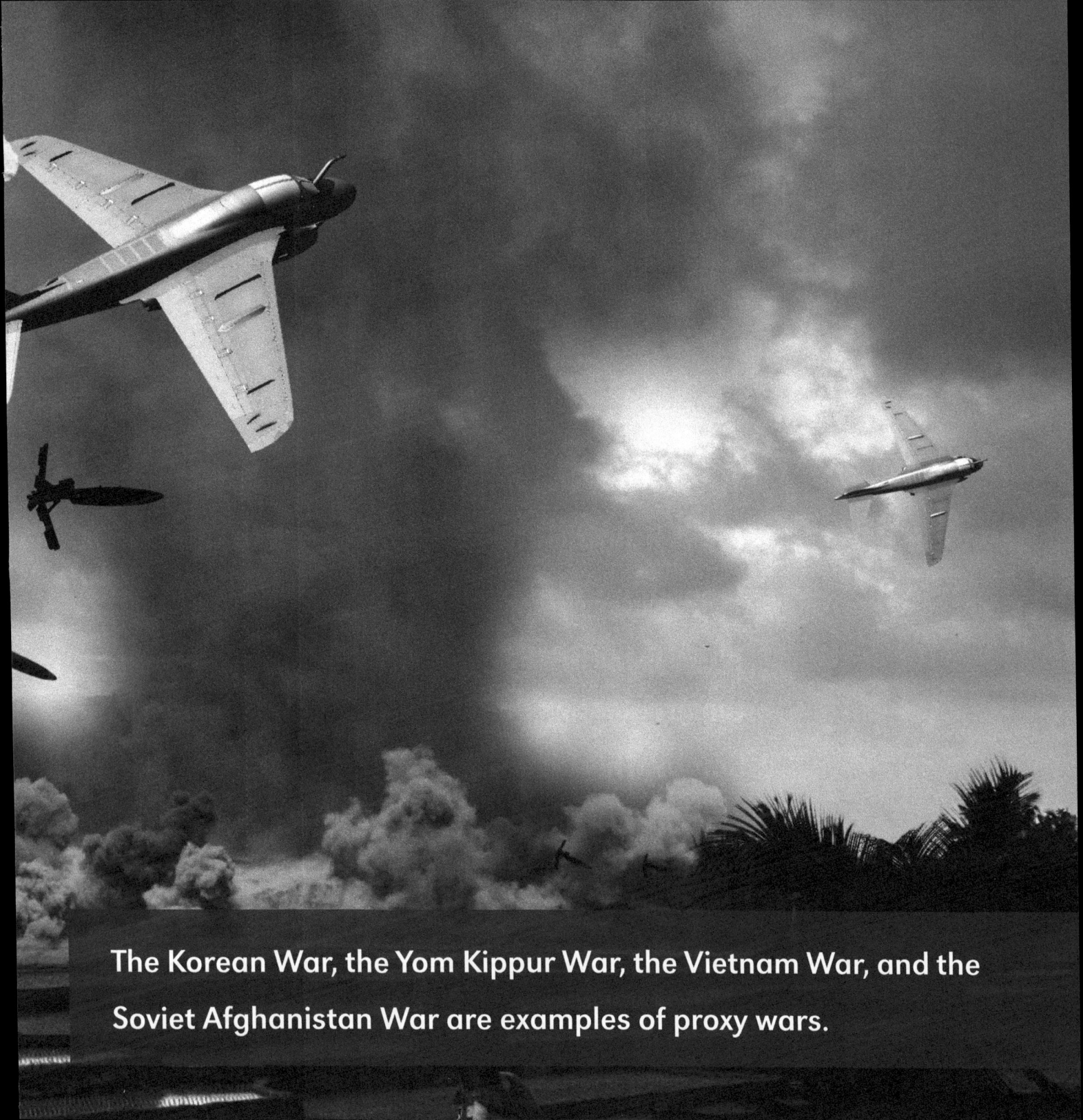

The Korean War, the Yom Kippur War, the Vietnam War, and the Soviet Afghanistan War are examples of proxy wars.

THE SPACE RACE AND THE ARMS RACE

The Soviet Union and the United States also tried fighting the Cold War by use of their technology and power. An example would be the Arms Race in which both sides tried having the greatest weapons as well as most nuclear bombs. This idea was having a huge weapons stockpile to deter the enemy from attacking.

The Space Race is another example, where each side wanted to show that they had the best technology and scientists by being first to achieve certain missions in space.

COMMUNISM

This is a form of philosophy and government and the goal is forming a society where everything is equally shared. Everyone is treated equally and there is very little private ownership. The government controls and owns almost everything including transportation, education, agriculture, means of production, as well as property.

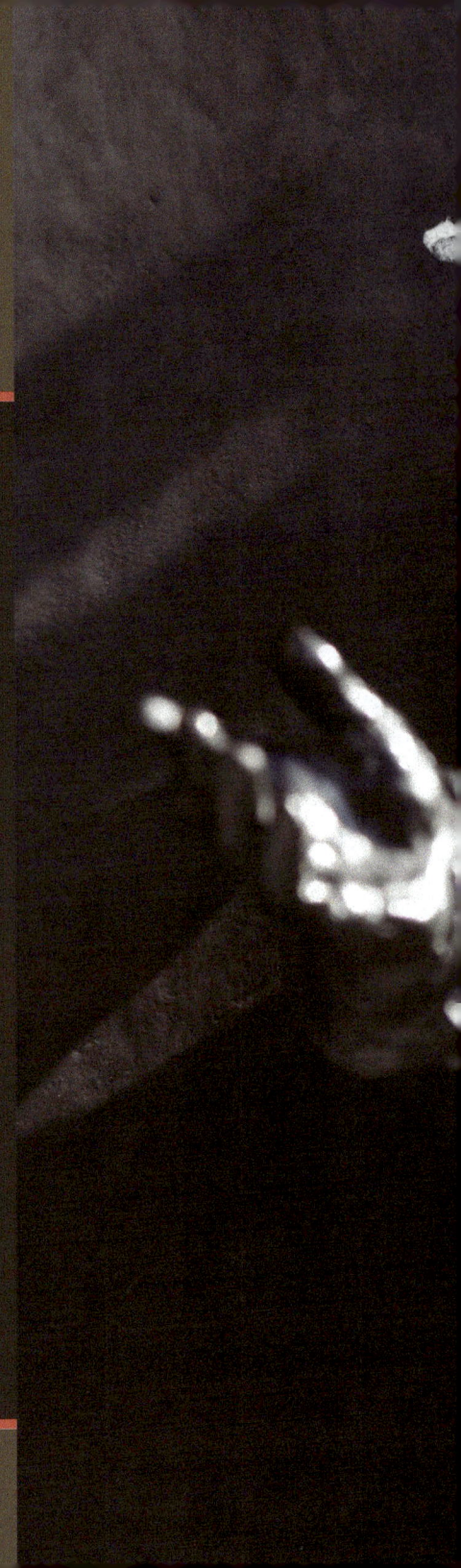

KARL HEINRICH MARX

HISTORY

Karl Marx is referred to as the Father of Communism. Marx was an economist and German philosopher who wrote his ideas in a book titled Communist Manifesto in 1848. His theories have been referred to as Marxism.

CAPITALISM

This is a form of economic system where a business may be owned privately and led by the people, other than by its government.

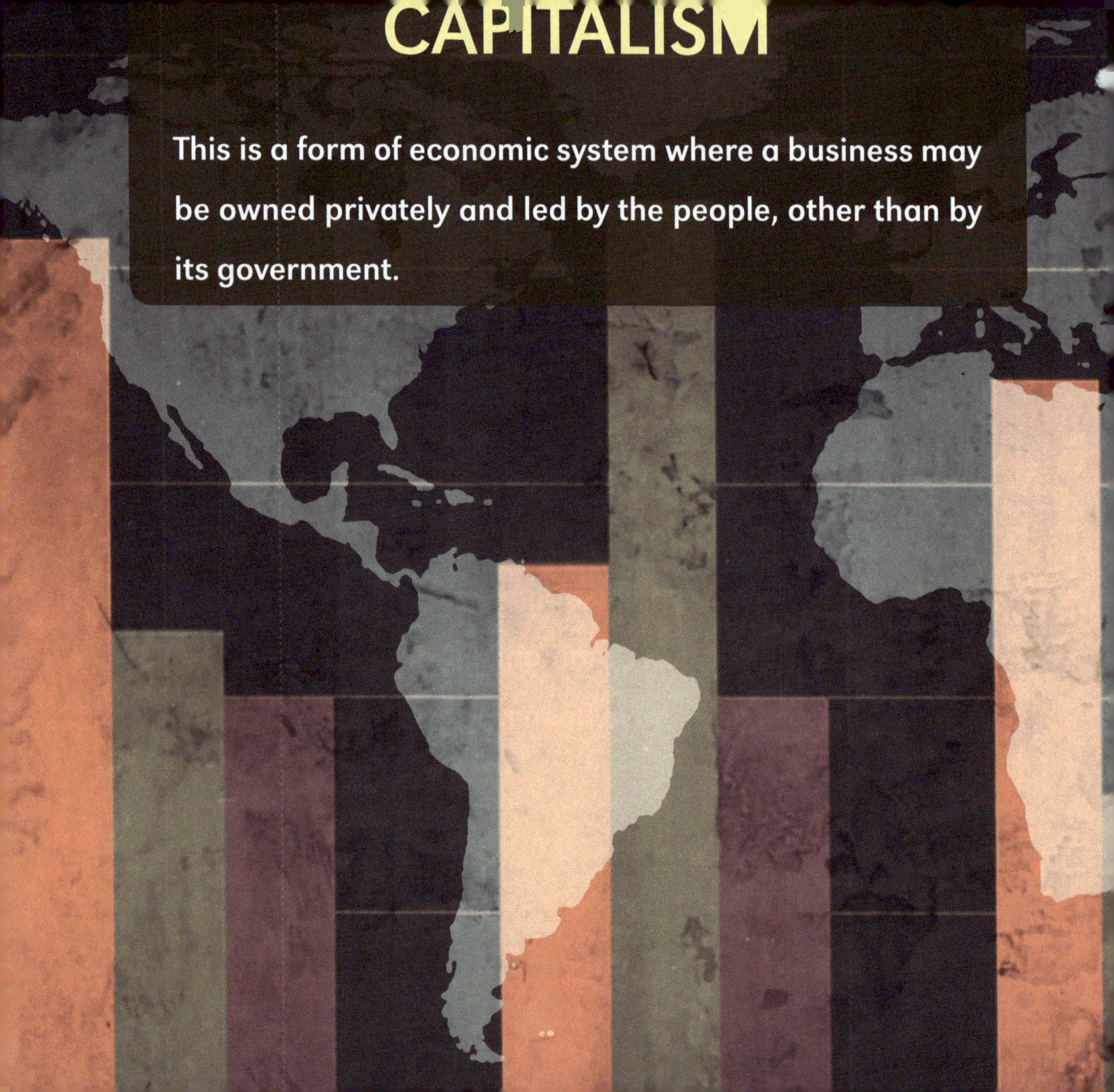

FREE MARKET

Capitalism is also known as the free-market system, where the word "free" indicates that a market can be free to work out its problems without any intervention by the government. A business can decide what products they would like to make as well as the price they would like to sell them for. People have the ability to choose what products they want to buy and what they want to pay for them.

SUPPLY AND DEMAND

This is one of the basic concepts of capitalism. Supply and demands provides that a product's price will settle at a point eventually where the product's demand equals the supply of the product.

ADAM SMITH

WHO WAS ADAM SMITH?

He was a Scottish economist whose idea about the free-market system was introduced first in 1776. The Wealth of Nations was a book he wrote describing how this type of economy would work. He believed that government should not interfere with the economy and competition should determine the pricing and products.

MODERN CAPITALISM

This idea differed somewhat from what Adam Smith had described.

STATUE OF ADAM SMITH

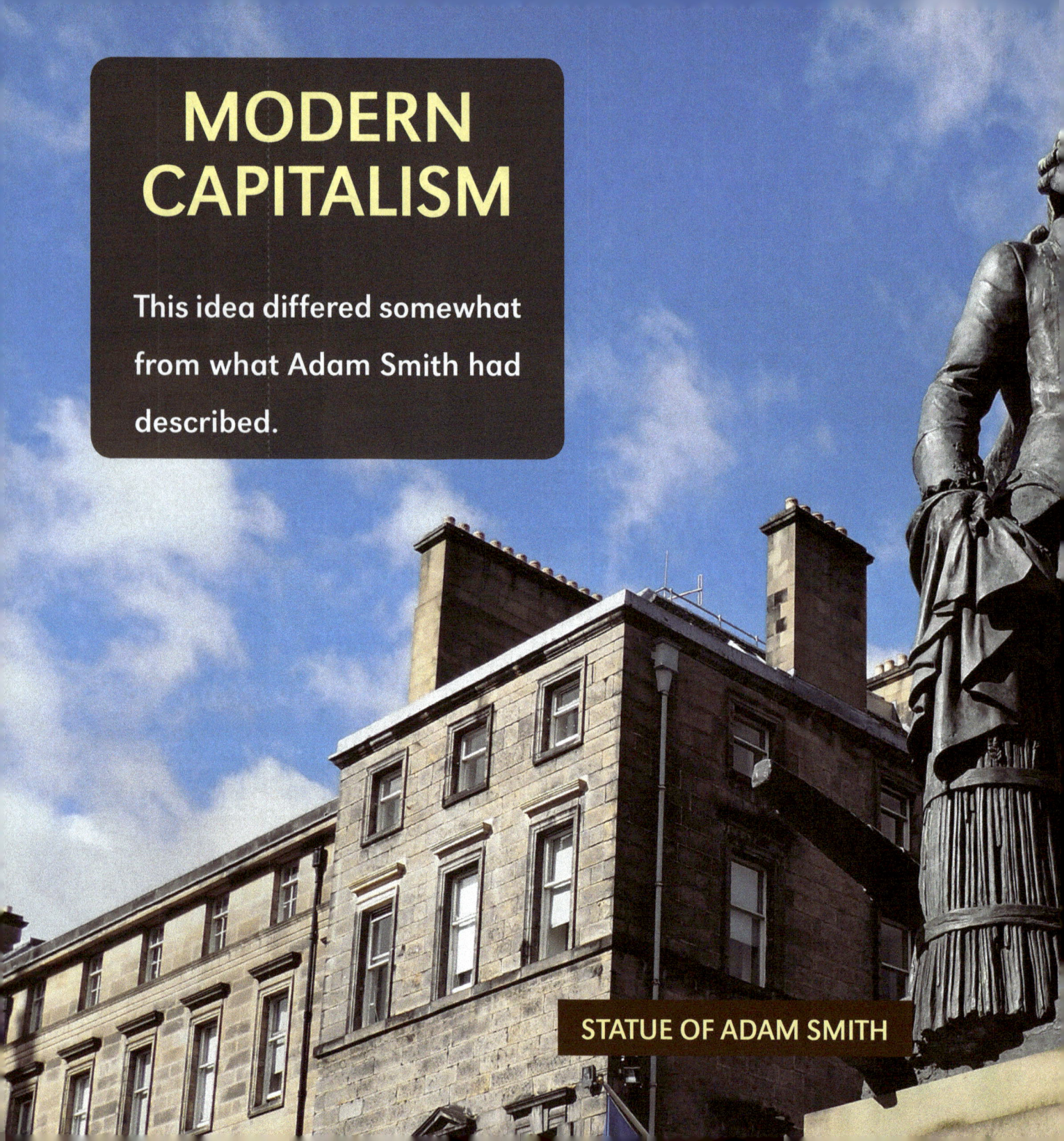

Several countries today have a capitalist economy, with the government taking a role in stabilizing their economy as well as providing regulations that provide protection for the public. This is known as a mixed economy.

The United States is an example of a capitalist economy. Government, however, has many laws monitoring the economy and businesses. Some of these laws are regulation for workplace safety, regulations for environmental protection, anti-discrimination laws, laws against monopolies, Social Security to protect the elderly, and taxes for redistribution of wealth. While most of the economy is run by capitalism, the government is involved quite a bit.

PROS AND CONS OF CAPITALISM

Some of the pros of capitalism include:

Efficiency - Capitalism forces one business to compete against another and this competition creates efficiency.

Freedom – In a capitalist economy, companies and people have the freedom to do whatever they choose and governments have less power and control which leads to a greater political freedom.

Innovation – Companies and people are both rewarded for innovation within a capitalist economy, which leads to more technological advances.

Economic Growth - Capitalism leads to a greater standard of living as well as economic growth.

Some of the cons of capitalism include:

Social inequality – Capitalism may lead to unfair distribution of wealth where a few people hold a great amount of the money.

Monopolies - Capitalism might create monopolies where a company can control supply and pricing without any intervention by the government.

Bad labor conditions - Capitalism may lead to working conditions that are unsafe as well as unfair wages for the working class.

There are many events that led up to the start of the Korean War and much more information about this war and the events that occurred after it ended. For additional information, you can visit your local library, research the internet, and ask questions of your teachers, family, and friends.

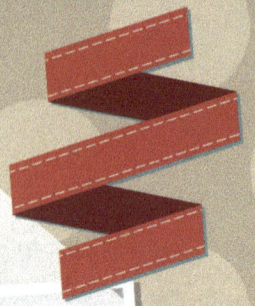

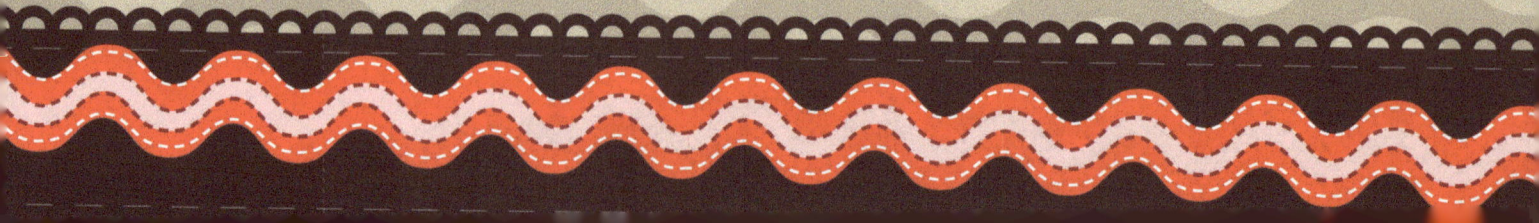

Visit

BABY PROFESSOR
EDUCATION KIDS

www.BabyProfessorBooks.com
to download Free Baby Professor eBooks
and view our catalog of new and exciting
Children's Books

Milton Keynes UK
Ingram Content Group UK Ltd.
UKHW050928310824
447642UK00002B/162

9 798869 415868